PROSPER ON PURPOSE

BY

DR. TAKETA WILLIAMS

PROSPER ON PURPOSE

ISBN 9781693008719
COPYRIGHT © IEXCEL ENTERPRISES LLC
WEBSITE: WWW.DRTAKETAWILLIAMS.ORG

PUBLISHED BY:
IEXCEL ENTERPRISES LLC
COLUMBUS, OHIO 43219

SCRIPTURE QUOTATIONS ARE USED PRIMARILY FROM THE KING JAMES VERSION
OF THE BIBLE, HOWEVER A FEW OTHER TRANSLATIONS ARE USED FROM VARIOUS
BIBLE VERSIONS.

PROSPERITY
is God's purpose for His people and the very thing that the devil fights against. The enemy does not want you to prosper. Satan's objective is to rob you of the life that Christ purposes for you to have. The Bible says according to John 10:10, "The thief cometh not, but for to steal, and to kill and to destroy: I am come that they might have life, and that they might have it more abundantly."

It is clear that the thief's ambition is to steal a life of abundance from you. An abundant life is a blessed, fruitful, prosperous and successful life. It is a rich, satisfying life that allows you live peacefully in the blessings of the Lord. According to Proverbs 10:22, "The blessing of the LORD, it maketh rich, and he addeth no sorrow with it." It is not the Will of God for you to live your days in pain and sorrow. The Lord wants you to prosper. Don't let the adversary bamboozle you out of your prosperous life. It's yours, possess it! Prosper on purpose.

WHAT IS PROSPERITY?

Prosperity is a condition of wholeness, complete fullness and a state of freedom from all manner of lack whereby nothing is missing, broken or lacking. Wholeness is to be unbroken and displays continuity. Continuity represents a continuous flow and progression. Prosperity causes one to progress and have good success.

"This Book of the Law shall not depart from your mouth, but you shall meditate in it day and night, that you may observe to do according to all that is written in it. For then you will make your way prosperous, and then you will have good success." -Joshua 1:8 NKJV

Prosperity also means to experience gain, increase, growth and success. Prosperity is a demonstration of The Lord's Goodness and a manifestation good things, benefits and bountiful blessings.

In the Hebrew language, the word prosperity is 'tsalach' and means to prosper, advance, move forward and make great accomplishments. We see this type of prosperity in the life of Joseph, the Dreamer. The bible says in Genesis 39:3, "And his master saw that the Lord was with him and the Lord made all that he did to prosper in his hand." The Lord blessed Joseph to experience prosperity in the midst of adversity.

In Latin, the word for prosperity is 'prosperitas'. The meaning is to advance or gain in anything good or desirable and the attainment of a desired goal. It also means to experience successful progress in any business or enterprise.

May the Lord cause your business, your visions, your dreams, your career and all that you set your heart to do to prosper. May you greatly progress, achieve, and supersede every goal. May you receive back double for all that you have lost over the years and gain more than you've ever had before.

GOD'S PROMISE OF PROSPERITY

God's Word promises prosperity to those that obey and serve The Lord.

"If they obey and serve him, they shall spend their days in prosperity, and their years in pleasures." Job 36:11

IT'S GOD'S WILL FOR YOU TO PROSPER!

The Lord wants you to prosper. What true father wouldn't want his children to be blessed? Exactly, none! God is our Father and He desires to prosper you, bless you and cause great success to happen for you. It's His will for your life. According to the Word of God, your prosperity is God's priority.

"Beloved, I wish above all things that thou mayest prosper and be in health, even as thy soul prospereth."
-3 John 2

4

DECLARE
YOUR PROSPERITY

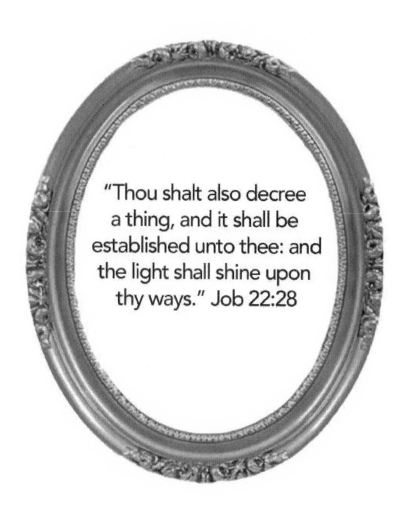

"Thou shalt also decree a thing, and it shall be established unto thee: and the light shall shine upon thy ways." Job 22:28

POWERFUL
PROSPERITY DECLARATIONS

Father, I boldly confess that it is
Your will for me to prosper.
Your Word says that You delight
Yourself in the prosperity
of Your servant. **Psalm 35:27**

I decree and declare that I prosper and shall be in good health even as my soul prospers.
3 John 2

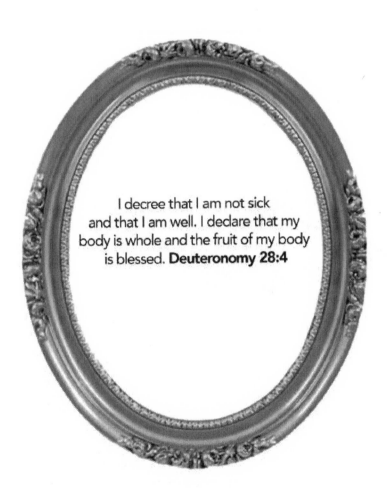

I decree that I am not sick and that I am well. I declare that my body is whole and the fruit of my body is blessed. **Deuteronomy 28:4**

I confess and believe that
Jesus Christ, who was rich, was made
poor for me, that I, through His
poverty may be made rich. I declare
that I am not poor and that I am wealthy.
2 Corinthians 8:9

Lord, I meditate upon
Your Word. I delight in Your Word
and declare that I am like a tree planted
by the rivers of water. My leaves shall
not wither. I shall bring forth fruit in it's
season and whatever I do
shall prosper.

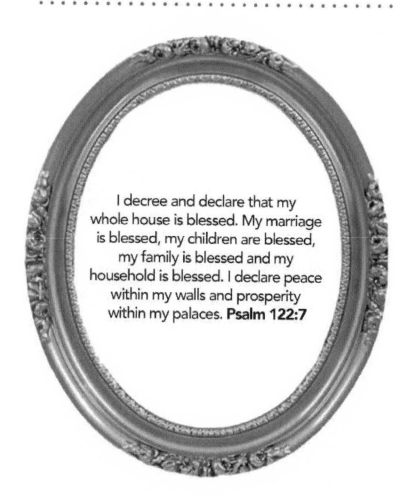

I decree and declare that my whole house is blessed. My marriage is blessed, my children are blessed, my family is blessed and my household is blessed. I declare peace within my walls and prosperity within my palaces. **Psalm 122:7**

POWERFUL
PROSPERITY DECLARATIONS

I declare that I don't live in frustration and I live in the peace of God. I decree that with a long, healthy, blessed, prosperous life God will satisfy me. **Psalm 91:16**

POWERFUL
PROSPERITY DECLARATIONS

I boldly declare
that I am an achiever and
failure is not an option for me
because I can do all things through
Christ that strengthens me,
(Philippians 4:13). I have been given
the ability to overcome and
succeed and therefore
I prosper. In Jesus' Name

I decree and declare that I am not defeated and I have victory over all manner of lack. Because the Lord is my Shepherd, I shall not want. I declare that I lack nothing. **Psalm 23:1**

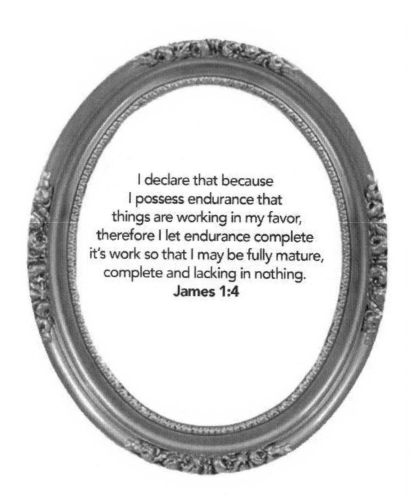

I declare that because
I possess endurance that
things are working in my favor,
therefore I let endurance complete
it's work so that I may be fully mature,
complete and lacking in nothing.
James 1:4

I declare that I prosper in my mind, in my body, in my spirit, and in my finances. I decree and declare complete wholeness because my faith has made me whole. **Luke 17:19**

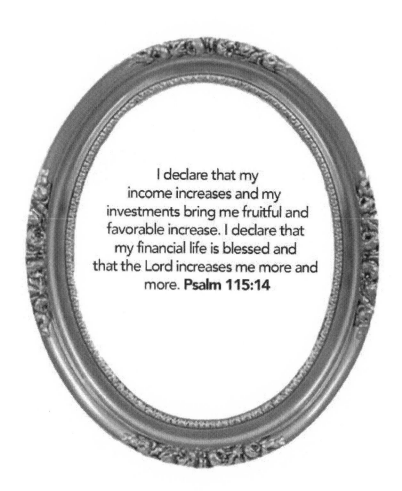

I declare that my income increases and my investments bring me fruitful and favorable increase. I declare that my financial life is blessed and that the Lord increases me more and more. **Psalm 115:14**

I declare miracle money,
miracle increase, miracle blessings
and miracle surprises are released
unto me now. **Job 9:10**

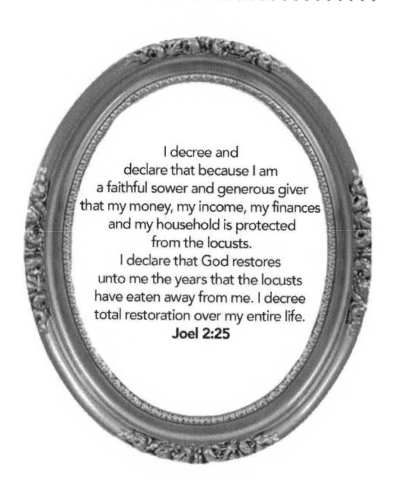

I decree and
declare that because I am
a faithful sower and generous giver
that my money, my income, my finances
and my household is protected
from the locusts.
I declare that God restores
unto me the years that the locusts
have eaten away from me. I decree
total restoration over my entire life.
Joel 2:25

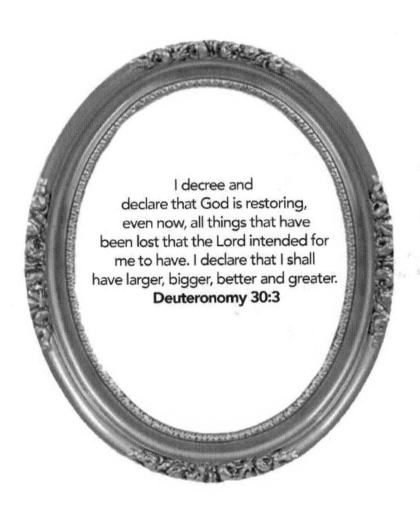

I decree and
declare that God is restoring,
even now, all things that have
been lost that the Lord intended for
me to have. I declare that I shall
have larger, bigger, better and greater.
Deuteronomy 30:3

I declare that God has
prepared a table before me and
that I shall eat good
in the face of all my enemies. I take
my seat at the table and shall eat in
plenty all the days of my life.
Psalm 23:5

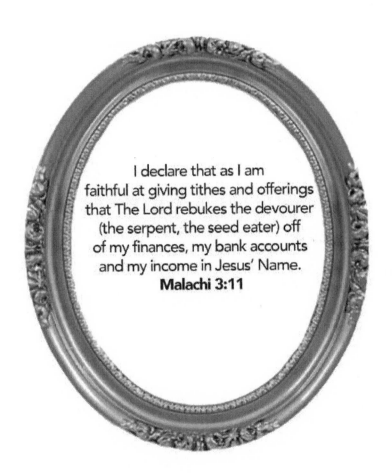

I declare that as I am
faithful at giving tithes and offerings
that The Lord rebukes the devourer
(the serpent, the seed eater) off
of my finances, my bank accounts
and my income in Jesus' Name.
Malachi 3:11

POWERFUL
PROSPERITY DECLARATIONS

I declare that
I prosper in my marriage,
my relationships, my friendships
and in every area of my life. Whatever
I do it prospers. I decree and declare that
God is touching the hearts of kings and
causing the wealthy to open up their
hands to me. **Proverbs 21:1**

POWERFUL
PROSPERITY DECLARATIONS

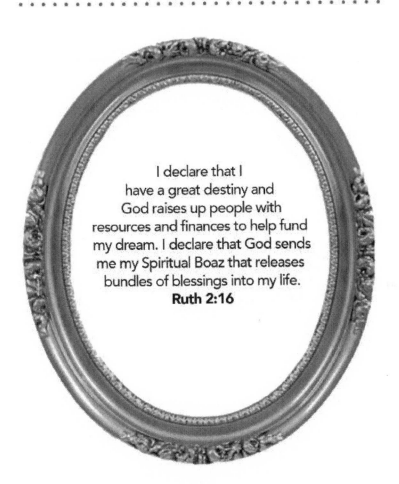

I declare that I
have a great destiny and
God raises up people with
resources and finances to help fund
my dream. I declare that God sends
me my Spiritual Boaz that releases
bundles of blessings into my life.
Ruth 2:16

POWERFUL
PROSPERITY DECLARATIONS

I decree and
declare money, finances, wealth
and favour is being multiplied
in my life even now. **In Jesus' Name**

POWERFUL
PROSPERITY DECLARATIONS

I declare that I will **never** be broke another day in my life and that God always provides my **every** need.

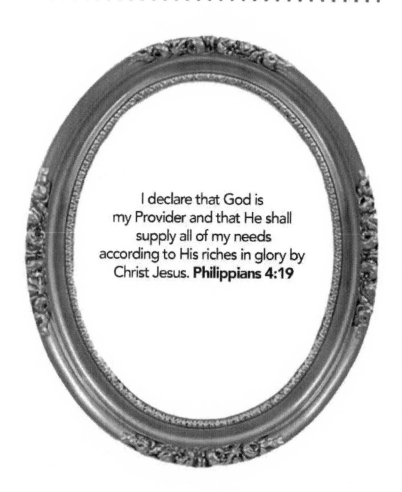

I declare that God is
my Provider and that He shall
supply all of my needs
according to His riches in glory by
Christ Jesus. **Philippians 4:19**

I declare that as
I have given, it shall be given
back unto me, good
measure, pressed down, shaken
together and running over. I decree
and declare that I have an abundant
supply. **Luke 6:38**

I declare that God is shifting me from running out to running over. The blessing of sustainment is upon me and I do not run out of anything.
2 Kings 4:6

I declare that the floodgates of heaven are opened over me and I shall receive a blessing that I cannot contain. I decree my next blessing will be enormous. It will be huge. **Malachi 3:10**

POWERFUL PROSPERITY DECLARATIONS

I confess that
I walk in God's favour today in all
my business dealings and
with people. God's favour rests
upon me. I have God's favour
greatly upon me and His blessings
surround me. **Psalm 5:12**

POWERFUL
PROSPERITY DECLARATIONS

I declare that God
gives me preferential treatment
and that this is my day to
receive extraordinary favour.
God's special favour is upon me now.
He makes His face to shine
upon me. He is gracious to me.
I expect something good to
happen to me and for me today.
Luke 2:52 and Numbers 6:25-26

I declare that God delights in my success and prosperity. It pleases God to bless me. I magnify The Lord and therefore He strongly desires for me to prosper. **Psalm 35:27**

POWERFUL
PROSPERITY DECLARATIONS

I declare that with
God all things are possible,
therefore today I am
expecting God's favour and success
to be upon me. **Mark 9:23**

POWERFUL
PROSPERITY DECLARATIONS

I decree and declare
that I am blessed. I am blessed
coming in and blessed going out.
I am the head and not the tail,
I am above only and not beneath.
I declare that I live on top.
Deuteronomy 28:2-14

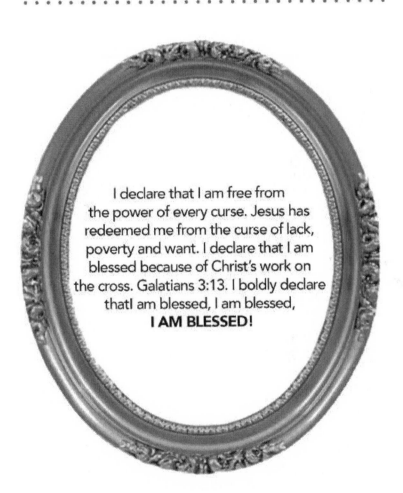

I declare that I am free from
the power of every curse. Jesus has
redeemed me from the curse of lack,
poverty and want. I declare that I am
blessed because of Christ's work on
the cross. Galatians 3:13. I boldly declare
thatI am blessed, I am blessed,
I AM BLESSED!

RADICAL FAITH PRAYER

Lord, I thank you that you have dealt unto me a measure of faith (Romans 12:3) and that my faith has increased because I have heard your Word (Romans 10:17). I confess that I have Radical Faith and that my faith does not waiver in hard times. Without faith it is impossible to please You (Hebrews 11:6). I confess that my faith, my lifestyle and my ways are pleasing to You. I believe that Jesus is Lord and that God You reign above every situation and circumstance. I believe Your Word is truth and I do not doubt even in my darkest moment. I have faith that your Word is a lamp unto my feet and a light to my path (Psalm 119:105). I have faith that you will lead me and guide me even when I can't see my way through. Lord in all things I trust you with all my heart and I will not lean to my own understanding, but in all my ways I will acknowledge you and you promised you would direct my path (Proverbs 3:5). I will not try to figure everything out on my own, but I will trust in Your ability to carry me through hard places and tumultuous times.

Lord bring stability to my journey and make all crooked places along my pathway straight. Make the foundation of my life firm, steady, steadfast and strong. Teach me to hold up the shield of faith because I realize the only thing that will keep me is Your Word and My Faith. When the adversary throws flaming arrows at me, allow my faith to quench every fiery dart of the enemy (Ephesians 6:16). Allow my faith to put out every flame and extinguish every fire, In Jesus' Name,. I choose to live a radical, faith-filled life for Your glory. Father I surrender and submit my faith to Your work and to Your will and the work of God is to believe (John 6:29). I will trust in Your Word and have Radical Faith like Moses to face my Rea Sea with boldnessand courage knowing that You will open the way, drive back the waters and bring me through with mighty victory. I declare that the sea will not drown me, but will swallow up all my enemies.

I declare that I have Radical Faith like the woman with the issue of blood who took a great risk and pressed her way into Your presence to touch the hem of Your garment. As I pull on You Jesus, let Your Virtue, Your Anointing be released in my life to destroy every yoke of evil, poverty and infirmity.

Lord You said in Your Word that all things are possible to him that believeth (Mark 9:23); therefore, because I possess Radical Faith, give me immediate victory over all impossibilities. Nothing shall be impossible unto me. I can do all things through Christ that strengthens me (Philippians 4:13).

Lord You are my light and my salvation, whom shall I fear? The Lord is the stronghold of my life of whom shall I be afraid (Psalm 27:1)? In the day of trouble, You will keep me safe, You will shelter me inside the secret and set me high upon a rock. You are my Refuge and my Fortress and in You will I trust (Psalm 91:2). I will not be afraid; I will only trust in You. You are my Source, You are my Strength, You are my Peace, You are my Protector and You are my Provider. I believe in You with my whole heart.

Now unto Him who is able to do exceeding abundantly above all I can ask or think according to the power that works in me (Ephesians 3:20). I declare that my Radical Faith is releasing Your Radical Power and Radical Prosperity in my life. Lord through Your Radical Power at work in me, do Radical Things for me. Cause Radical Blessings to fall fresh on me, on my family, on my children, on my household, on my health, on my finances, on my career, on my business and on everything that I have. Cause Radical Restoration, Radical Miracles, Radical Breakthroughs and Radical Turnarounds to manifest for me NOW. Send NOW prosperity (Psalm 118:25). Give me back everything that I lost and everything the devil stole from me 100-Fold (Mark 10:30). I have the faith to receive it all back. I want what's mine; therefore, I give you what's Yours. I GIVE YOU RADICAL FAITH. Lord God, cause me to prosper on purpose.

In the Mighty, Magnificent, Matchless Name of Jesus I Pray, Amen

Made in the USA
Middletown, DE
12 April 2022

64080663R00024